POLAROIDS OF WOMEN

DEWEY NICKS

T. ADLER BOOKS, SANTA BARBARA

Stephanie & Dewey Nicks, Hollywood

The past is a fickle place. It feels both like yesterday and a million years ago.

In the pre-digital age, Polaroids were used to test light and composition before committing something to film. They were fast and immediate, considered utilitarian. Often dozens were shot before all was ready for the "real" camera. Most of the time those Polaroids were tossed, but Dewey saved his favorites. Others were discarded or resigned to refrigerator fronts and bankers boxes, backs of drawers, and scrapbooks. Polaroid images fade fast, they yellow and crack. They are not archival.

Dewey had great affection for stylish architecture and interiors and for a more glamorous past of classic cars and resort style living, tube amps and highballs, everything custom. When he needed locations we would brainstorm and wish list. We were both interested in iconic and, in those days, under appreciated California, Hawaii, and New York locations. A lot of the time we just used the excuse of a photo shoot to get inside places and meet people we had long admired and were still alive (i.e. Paul Rudolph's Beekman Place penthouse or Albert Frey's modernist hillside aerie in Palm Springs). Often the location would not even show up in the final edit but the inspiration and relaxation of being there sure did.

In some ways these Polaroids have more authenticity than what ultimately ran in the ads or editorials. The subjects knew when Dewey was shooting "for real" but in these Polaroids the women look more relaxed, not quite yet turning it completely "on." And being on set with Dewey is legendary. He is an old school master storyteller and impressionist, seriously one of the funniest people I have ever met. His shoots were hard work but you were very entertained. The girls loved him. He was always, every minute, fully engaged.

They are like ice cubes these memories, these Polaroids—frozen in time moments on paper, fragile, melting, fading, on their way out. They can be gorgeous, especially at this stage of their disintegration, with the chemically imperfect edges and soft Outerbridge-like muted colors. I like that he is scanning and publishing now, freezing them again at this later, different, softer stage of their lifespan, for posterity. They are as beautiful as can be and they trigger the fondest memories.

The photos may fade but memory is more permanent than ink.

– Brad Dunning

Bijou Phillips & Emily Cadenhead, Palm Springs

Julia Stiles, Morgan House, Hollywood

Shalom Harlow, 12th Street, New York

Lindsey & Amanda Lockwood, Sunset Strip, West Hollywood

Diane Lane, Stone Canyon

Isaac Mizrahi & Shalom Harlow, New York

Shalom Harlow, New York

Sandra Taylor, Morgan House, Hollywood

Angela Lindvall, Manhattan

Salma Hayek, Culver City

Carré Otis, New York

Hanalei Bay, Kauai

Morgan House, Hollywood

Ingrid Seynhaeve & Valeria Mazza, Kona

Jasmine Guinness, Zuma Beach

Valeria Mazza, Morgan House, Hollywood

Kristina Semenovskaia, Stone Canyon

Ruza Madarevic, Wexler Steel House, Palm Springs

Morgan House, Hollywood

Sara Lamm, Montauk

Cambria, California

Ruza Madarevic, Wexler Steel House, Palm Springs

Jaime Rishar, Palm Springs

Myka Dunkle, Culver City

Minnie Driver, Bel Air

Noemi de Kwiatkowski, Manhattan

Noemi de Kwiatkowski, Manhattan

Myka Dunkle, Culver City

Patricia Arquette, Hollywood

Tanga Moreau, Naples Ranch, California

Tanga Moreau, Naples Ranch, California

Cindy Crawford, Big Sur

Valeria Mazza, Kona

Ruza Madarevic, Wexler Steel House, Palm Springs

Marianne Schröder, Hollywood

Jordan Ladd, Inglewood

Carla Gugino, Bel Air

Lisa Storey, Jenny Levy & Pati Dubroff, Silver Lake

Lisa Storey & Pati Dubroff, Silver Lake

Natalie Portman, Hell's Kitchen, New York

Natalie Portman, Upper East Side, New York

Elizabeth Berkley, Morgan House, Hollywood

Elizabeth Berkley, Morgan House, Hollywood

Leilani Bishop, Zuma Beach

Shirley Mallmann & Nathalie Love, Malibu

Shalom Harlow, New York

Sara Lamm, Montauk

Kristina Semenovskaia, Bel Air

Kristina Semenovskaia, Bel Air

Josie Perez, Morgan House, Hollywood

Patricia Arquette, Morgan House, Hollywood

Heather Graham, Bel Air

Ingrid Seynhaeve & Valeria Mazza, Diamond Head, Hawaii

Nathalie Love, Stone Canyon

Nikki Uberti, Bel Air

Meghan Douglas, Paris

Jasmine Guinness, Zuma Beach

Angela Lindvall, Manhattan

Julia Stiles, Morgan House, Hollywood

Nikki Uberti, Bel Air

Ingrid Seynhaeve, Diamond Head, Hawaii

Meghan Douglas, New York

Michele Hicks, Wexler Steel House, Palm Springs

Jaime Rishar, Palm Springs

Jaime Rishar, Palm Springs

Valeria Mazza, Honolulu

Amber Valletta, Joshua Tree

Missy Gibson, Laguna Beach

Patricia Arquette, Hollywood

Angela Lindvall, New York

Lisa Eisner, New York

Morgan House, Hollywood

Ingrid Seynhaeve & Valeria Mazza, Kona

Niki Taylor, Miami Beach

Anna Klevhag, Palm Springs

Pasadena

Josie Perez & Mark Fisher, Central Park

Jaime King, Beverly Hills

Cindy Crawford, Big Sur

Anna Klevhag, Palm Springs

Ruza Madarevic, Wexler Steel House, Palm Springs

Pomona Freeway

Milla Jovovich, LAX

Nessie Gitlis-Graizon, Wexler Steel House, Palm Springs

Sofia Coppola, Morgan House, Hollywood

Jasmine Guinness, Zuma Beach

Brandi Quinones, Malibu

Jaime Rishar, Morgan House, Hollywood

Silver Lake

Nicola Vassell, Palm Springs

Nessie Gitlis-Graizon, Wexler Steel House, Palm Springs

Larissa Bondarenko, Palm Springs

Sofia Coppola, Morgan House, Hollywood

Kristen McMenamy, Greenwich Village, New York

Cher, Hollywood

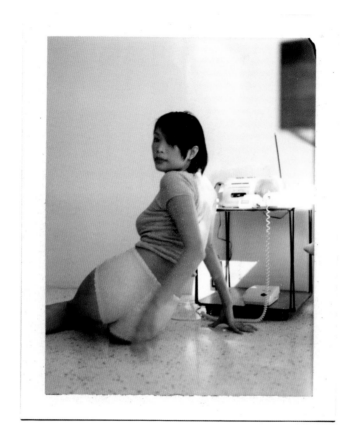

Navia Nguyen, Wexler Steel House, Palm Springs

Navia Nguyen, Wexler Steel House, Palm Springs

Cambria, California

Jenna Elfman, Zuma Beach

Milla Jovovich, New York

Leilani Bishop, Palm Springs

Jasmine Guinness, Zuma Beach

Sara Lamm, Montauk

Pati Dubroff, Silver Lake

Jenny Levy, Silver Lake

Donald Wexler Steel House, Palm Springs

Donald Wexler Steel House, Palm Springs

Irving Gill's Morgan House, Hollywood

Irving Gill's Morgan House, Hollywood

ACKNOWLEDGEMENTS

Dedicated to Stephanie Nicks, the beautiful woman who shares her life with me.

A heartfelt thank you to Henry Wei Han whose support and assistance is treasured.

My gratitude goes out to the people who made this book possible. Tom Adler, Brad Dunning, Carol LeFlufy, Barrett Schultz, Mandy Zika, Mario Fuentes, and Merle Ginsberg.

To all the cherished collaborators who have invested their time, talent, and energy into the images of this book, I hope you find the memories as gorgeous and precious as I do.

First edition published by T. Adler Books, Santa Barbara

Copyright © 2018 Dewey Nicks

Copyright © 2018 Foreword by Brad Dunning

Design & edit by T. Adler Books

Research & production by Mandy Zika

Distributed by D.A.P. / Distributed Art Publishers

New York, New York, U.S.A.

Printed in China (ICLA)

ISBN 978-1-942884-34-7